Lessons from the Master Teacher

An Educator's Journey with Jesus

Brea Ratliff

Copyright © 2017 Brea C. Ratliff

All scripture from the World English Bible unless otherwise specified

All rights reserved.

ISBN-13: 978-1976394102

ISBN-10: 1976394104

DEDICATION

This book is a compilation of many things God has revealed to me over several years of being an educator. I am truly grateful for the ability to glean wisdom and knowledge for my life from the experiences of Jesus.

I believe teaching is an honorable profession, and the parallels between Jesus' experience and my own have given me peace and strength as I continue to grow—both as a professional and a believer.

I dedicate this book to my family and the many amazing mentors, teachers and students I've had throughout my life.

To the reader, I thank you for allowing me to share with you the joys, the missteps, and the lessons I've learned from walking in fellowship with Jesus Christ, the Master Teacher.

CONTENTS

	Introduction	i
1	Christ – The Hope of Glory	1
2	Attitude is Everything	10
3	The Character of the Master Teacher	18
4	Promoting Conceptual Understanding	27
5	Differentiated Instruction	35
6	Engage and Persevere	43
7	Investing with Expectation	51
8	The Power of Words	59
9	Checking for Understanding	65
10	Instructional Coaching	71
11	Setting Expectations for Excellence	77
12	The Company We Keep	85
13	Give It Your All	90
	Bibliography	95

INTRODUCTION

^{35} Again, the next day, John was standing with two of his disciples, ^{36} and he looked at Jesus as he walked, and said, "Behold, the Lamb of God!" ^{37} The two disciples heard him speak, and they followed Jesus.
^{38} Jesus turned, and saw them following, and said to them, "What are you looking for?"
They said to him, "Rabbi" (which is to say, being interpreted, Teacher), "where are you staying?"
^{39} He said to them, "Come, and see." They came and saw where he was staying, and they stayed with him that day. It was about the tenth hour.
^{40} One of the two who heard John, and followed him, was Andrew, Simon Peter's brother.

> ⁴¹ *He first found his own brother, Simon, and said to him, "We have found the Messiah!" (which is, being interpreted, Christ).* (John 1:35-41)

The early disciples and their leader, John, often referred to as John the Baptist, had long awaited the arrival of the Messiah. Often interrogated by his contemporaries about his own role and position in the kingdom of God (John 1:19-28), John responds to these queries by referencing the centuries-old prophecy of Isaiah, and declaring the Messiah was soon to come.

> ²⁶ *John answered them, "I baptize in water, but among you stands one whom you don't know.*
> ²⁷ *He is the one who comes after me, who is preferred before me, whose sandal strap I'm not worthy to loosen."* (John 1:26-27)

In the days following this declaration, John and other men acknowledged Jesus as the Messiah and Lamb of God. These men professed Jesus to be a rabbi, while also expressing a sincere desire to follow Him. Jesus responds to their request by calling his future disciples to "Come, and see" (John 1:39), which meant more than simply coming to see where He was staying at that time. It was an invitation for those men to come and learn more about Him in the completeness of who He is.

"Rabbi" is a term which means "Jewish scholar or teacher." In that day and culture, individuals identified as rabbis were often physicians, or highly educated men in a field of knowledge. Recognizing Jesus as a rabbi is the equivalent of calling him *master* or more specifically, *teaching master*.

Through His teaching, Jesus revealed the complexity of who He is beyond being the "image of the invisible God" (Colossians 1:15) and "the way, the truth, and the life" (John 14:6) for our salvation. Jesus used His diverse teaching ministry to revolutionize the world: promoting God's love for humanity and challenging the fixed mindsets and beliefs of an entire generation.

Using approaches condemned by His contemporaries as controversial, Jesus announced a radical new message of faith, hope, redemption, and freedom to all people. He refused to abide by societal rules, and instructed all those who came to Him; individuals with wealth and influence, as well as those cast aside by society as poor or of lesser value.

Over the past seventeen years, I have had the unique opportunity to teach and lead in both traditional and non-traditional settings. I have served as an adjunct professor and mathematics education research coordinator with Southern Methodist University, a K-12 district mathematics supervisor, a high school mathematics/science academic coach, and I have taught mathematics on every grade level.

Through each experience, I've learned how studying the dynamic life of the Master Teacher has led me to foundational truth about what effective teaching and learning should look like. I find joy in my own experience and strength to endure the challenges of teaching when I reflect on the example Jesus set before us. His life validates the importance of teaching as a ministry. The lessons taught by Jesus are an invaluable gift, and as educators, we have the honor and great responsibility to continue this work.

I invite every education professional to "Come, and see" the Holy Scriptures in a new way. Examine the beautiful alignment between the life of the Master Teacher and what we have been called to do as believers who are educators.

Brea Ratliff

1

CHRIST – THE HOPE OF GLORY

¹¹ For no one can lay any other foundation than that which has been laid, which is Jesus Christ. (1 Corinthians 3:11)

One of my favorite hymns is "The Solid Rock" written by Edward Mote. I was very young when I first learned the song, but understood the lyrics were assurance that as I trusted in Him, Jesus Christ would always be the foundation of my life. He would provide stability and peace within an unpredictable world; one Edward Mote (NBPB, 1977) declares to be as precarious as "sinking sand."

Even though I developed a deep and fulfilling relationship with the Lord, it was years before I could fully comprehend why Christ was attached to Jesus' name.

The Anointed One Lives in You

The name "Christ" means "the anointed one." Jesus was the anointed One of God. The Bible explains how Jesus came as God in the flesh, and lived among us as a man who used the special authority of God to accomplish powerful supernatural works (Winston, 2017). The amazing and beautiful revelation is that for every believer, this same anointing of God lives inside of us. The *same* anointing which guided and directed Jesus throughout his life on earth is available to you and me every day.

> *25 God has sent me to help his Church and to tell his secret plan to you Gentiles. 26-27 He has kept this secret for centuries and generations past, but now at last it has pleased him to tell it to those who love him and live for him, and the riches and glory of his plan are for you Gentiles, too. And this is the*

secret: **Christ in your hearts is your only hope of glory.**

²⁸ *So everywhere we go we talk about Christ to all who will listen, warning them and teaching them as well as we know how. We want to be able to present each one to God, perfect because of what Christ has done for each of them.* ²⁹ *This is my work, and I can do it only because Christ's mighty energy is at work within me. (Colossians 1: 25-29, The Living Bible)*

These verses opened my eyes to a new revelation concerning Christ and the foundation of my faith.

To those who don't know Jesus, the way God works through his Holy Spirit remains a mystery, but to those who believe, it is the key to abundant life.

The anointed One is the Holy Spirt of God which lives inside of us; constantly working in and through us to produce heaven on earth (Winston, 2017). The Holy Spirit confers the knowledge, power and wisdom of God upon every believer, *but we must believe.*

When Paul wrote to the church in Philippi, "I can do all things through Christ which strengtheneth me" (Philippians 4:13, King James Version), I struggled with the translation. Surely, there had been a typo: Why would the translator use the word "which" instead of "whom"? The answer is because Christ is the Holy Spirit—the anointing. Re-reading that verse in this context means it is the anointing which gives us strength to accomplish any and everything.

I have accessed the anointing of God many times throughout my life, and have seen supernatural things occur. I've spoken peace to natural (and spiritual) storms, and watched them recede. I've followed Jesus' instructions and laid hands on those who have been sick (Mark 16:18) as God healed their bodies. I've prayed for people and saw the Holy Spirit move on their behalf in miraculous ways. What I realized, however, was that I was not accessing the anointing of Christ every single day.

Did I *really* believe the anointing could impact change in my school, my city, my country, or the world? On a micro level, did I have the faith to believe that the Christ in me could overcome the challenging day-to-day interactions I had with my students, parents, and colleagues? I didn't always, but I do now. Christ within us equips every believer to be changed and affect change wherever we are.

We Have Power Through Christ

In his letter to the Corinthians, Paul explains the power and might of Christ at work in every believer:

> *10-13 The Spirit, not content to flit around on the surface, dives into the depths of God, and brings out what God planned all along. Who ever knows what you're thinking and planning except you*

yourself? The same with God—except that he not only knows what he's thinking, but he lets us in on it. God offers a full report on the gifts of life and salvation that he is giving us. We don't have to rely on the world's guesses and opinions. We didn't learn this by reading books or going to school; we learned it from God, who taught us person-to-person through Jesus, and we're passing it on to you in the same firsthand, personal way.

14-16 *The unspiritual self, just as it is by nature, can't receive the gifts of God's Spirit. There's no capacity for them. They seem like so much silliness. Spirit can be known only by spirit—God's Spirit and our spirits in open communion. Spiritually alive, we have access to everything God's Spirit is doing, and can't be judged by unspiritual critics. Isaiah's question, "Is there anyone around who knows God's Spirit, anyone who knows what he is doing?" has been* *answered: Christ knows, and we have Christ's Spirit.* (1 Corinthians 2: 10-16, The Message)

Jesus told us that we are to do greater works than those He completed *because* we have His spirit within us (John 14:10,12). Unfortunately, many believers feel uncertain about accessing the anointing, and think it can be taken away from them based on their behavior. This is a lie from Satan, who is the father of lies.

Believe that God has placed you in education to work through you by the Holy Spirit to bring about change in seemingly impossible situations. He is waiting on us to stand firm and know we can do all things through Christ.

An educator's prayer:

Father, I believe the same anointing which rested on Jesus now resides in me as a believer. I thank You for allowing me to be used as a vessel to accomplish your will in the earth. Help me to trust You, and remember that Your anointing—the Christ in me—cannot be taken away from me. I recognize that You have not given me a spirit of fear, but one of power, love, and a sound mind. By Your Holy Spirit, help me to demolish every stronghold and argument which threatens to destroy my confidence in You, and walk in the position You have placed me in. I believe I can do all things through Christ which gives me strength. In Jesus' name, Amen!

Lessons from the Master Teacher

Notes:

2
ATTITUDE IS EVERYTHING

When I first started teaching, I would reach a point in the year where I blamed my students' lack of progress on their poor attitudes about learning and school. I would often express my frustration to colleagues, family members and friends who would validate my feelings.

"Yeah, kids these days are just lazy."

"If they would put in the effort, you could actually teach!"

"It's the parents' fault. The parents don't care, so their kids don't care."

It was years before I understood how my own attitude and response to my students was contributing to this toxic cycle. Jesus showed me I have a responsibility in these situations too, and there's always more happening than what I observe and feel.

In the first chapter of John, Jesus meets several men who would later become His disciples. Through this account, we have an opportunity to witness the Master Teacher and His loving response to Nathaniel, a student with a cynical outlook.

Jesus Calls Philip and Nathanael

> ^{43} *On the next day, he was determined to go out into Galilee, and he found Philip. Jesus said to him, "Follow me."*
> ^{44} *Now Philip was from Bethsaida, of the city of Andrew and Peter.*
> ^{45} *Philip found Nathanael, and said to him, "We have found him, of whom Moses in the law, and the prophets, wrote: Jesus of Nazareth, the son of Joseph."*
> ^{46} *Nathanael said to him, "Can any good thing come out of Nazareth?"*
> *Philip said to him, "Come and see."*
> ^{47} *Jesus saw Nathanael coming to him, and said about him, "Behold, an Israelite*

indeed, in whom is no deceit!"
⁴⁸ Nathanael said to him, "How do you know me?"
Jesus answered him, "Before Philip called you, when you were under the fig tree, I saw you."
⁴⁹ Nathanael answered him, "Rabbi, you are the Son of God! You are King of Israel!"
⁵⁰ Jesus answered him, "Because I told you, 'I saw you underneath the fig tree,' do you believe? You will see greater things than these!"
⁵¹ He said to him, "Most certainly, I tell you, hereafter you will see heaven opened, and the angels of God ascending and descending on the Son of Man."
(John 1: 43-51)

Through this passage of Scripture, Jesus reminds us that we choose our responses to the attitudes and ideas of others. Jesus, in His omniscience, is fully aware of Nathanael's thoughts toward Him, but *He chooses* to greet him with respect. He knows that Nathanael's experiences have taught him to doubt the Messiah could come from a city like Nazareth, but He also knows Nathanael is a man of integrity. It is this approach that disarms Nathanael, and as Jesus begins to tell him what He knows and what lies ahead for him, we see the life and vision of one young man changed forever.

Have you made yourself aware of the ways past and/or present experiences have impacted how your students approach school?

Jesus displayed an attitude of complete submission to God as He was leading others. In John 5:19, Jesus proclaims that He did nothing outside of what the Father told Him to do, and sought constant guidance from Him. Jesus maintained an attitude of humility and remained open to instruction, even in light of his own authority as the Son of God.

I realized I was continually dissatisfied with my students because I struggled to release the hurt, anger, and frustration I felt when their actions did not align with my expectations. I had to learn how to adopt the mind of Christ in everything I do as an educator. Paul, in his letter to the Philippians, reminds them of this life principle:

> [1] *If there is therefore any exhortation in Christ, if any consolation of love, if any fellowship of the Spirit, if any tender mercies and compassion,*
> [2] *make my joy full, by being like-minded, having the same love, being of one accord, of one mind;*
> [3] *doing nothing through rivalry or through conceit, but in humility, each counting others better than himself;*
> [4] *each of you not just looking to his own things, but each of you also to the things of others.*
> [5] *Have this in your mind, which was also in Christ Jesus,*
> [6] *who, existing in the form of God, didn't consider equality with God a thing to be grasped,*
> [7] *but emptied himself, taking the form of a servant, being made in the likeness of men.* (Philippians 2:1-7)

We can follow in Jesus' footsteps by demonstrating humility, maintaining a teachable spirit, and choosing to appeal to the integrity in our students or others in our professional spaces. As Paul wrote in his letter to the church in Colossae,

> *[12] Put on therefore, as God's chosen ones, holy and beloved, a heart of compassion, kindness, lowliness, humility, and perseverance;*
> *[13] bearing with one another, and forgiving each other, if any man has a complaint against any; even as Christ forgave you, so you also do.*
> (Colossians 3:12-13)

Many of us became educators because we believe the possibilities for greatness increase exponentially when people have access to high quality education. The dialogue between Jesus and Nathanael reminds us that progress in this area often lies in both the teacher's response to the student *and* the student's confidence in the teacher.

In this moment with the Master Teacher, we become aware of how shifting our attitudes can disarm arguments, resolve conflict, open the door for new revelation, and establish trust.

An educator's prayer:

Lord, help me to show my students that I care about them, who they are, and what they know. I pray that I would have the mind of Christ in my professional interactions with students, colleagues, and other stakeholders. Give me divine wisdom as I appeal to the integrity of who you created each of them to be. In Jesus' name, Amen.

3
THE CHARACTER OF THE MASTER TEACHER

"Brrrrrrrriiinnnnng."

The bell signaling the end of lunchtime jolts Mr. Washington's fifth-grade students to attention as they begin lining up in front of the cafeteria doors. Mr. Washington is always punctual, and has arrived in the cafeteria early today. He is barely able to contain his excitement as thoughts about the amazing science lesson he has planned for the afternoon flood his mind.

As his students greet him with high-fives and stories about a fight that almost happened between two students during the lunch period, Mr. Washington notices that his colleague, Ms. Lincoln, has not arrived to pick up her fifth-grade class. While he is

Notes:

anxious to start his lesson on time, Mr. Washington knows the best thing to do is remain in the cafeteria to ensure Ms. Lincoln's students are supervised.

"She's hardly ever late," he thinks to himself. "I'm sure she just needed to stop by the restroom".

Ten minutes later, Ms. Lincoln has still not arrived, and the students are getting restless.

"Mr. Washington!" exclaims a student from Ms. Lincoln's class, "I really need to use the restroom! I feel like I'm going to be sick! May I please be excused from the cafeteria?" Immediately three other students yell out similar requests to leave the cafeteria, but before Mr. Washington can answer any of them, he sees a bag of chips sail past his arm and land squarely on the back of another student's head. It seems the fight that almost happened during lunch has begun.

As Mr. Washington spins around to determine who has thrown the bag of chips, a rumble of shouting, laughter, and loud conversations begins to erupt from the once calm group of students.

Mr. Washington swiftly steps between the

student who has thrown the bag of chips and the student on the receiving end of the brief food fight. He reaches out, firmly placing one hand on each student's shoulder, and loudly says one word:

"Enough."

Mr. Washington's commanding presence unruffles the once angry students. The stern look now showing on his face compels every student in his class to return to their expected position in line. Ms. Lincoln's students follow suit, and fall as quiet as church mice.

Suddenly, the cafeteria door swings open, breaking the silence, and Ms. Lincoln dashes through the door frame. "Mr. Washington," she says breathlessly, "thank you for watching my students! I was in a parent conference that ran late. I hope they weren't any trouble."

Mr. Washington glances at the now silent group of students who are watching him with some consternation. He smiles and gives a slight chuckle. "Trouble? Not at all. Glad I could help." Mr. Washington holds a brief conference with the two students involved in the scuffle, and scolds them for their behavior. He then turns to address the rest of the class.

"Well," he declares with a grin, "I'm ready to get back to class. How about you? There's a lot of learning still to be done today, and I can't wait for you to see what I've got planned for our science lesson!" Almost immediately, the young men and women in Mr. Washington's class squeal with delight. The drama of the last 10 to 15 minutes quickly becomes a distant memory, as the class files into the hallway and begins walking eagerly back toward their classroom.

Many educators can relate to Mr. Washington's lunchroom experience. In fact, you may have a similar experience every day! Educators are trained to know how to handle interruptions—from minor crises to full-blown emergencies—all while being responsible for the safety of their students. The sheer magnitude of this responsibility means the ability to command peace and remain rational during any stressful situation is imperative. Let's look to the Master

Teacher for an example of His commanding presence.

Jesus Calms the Storm

> ³⁵ *On that day, when evening had come, he said to them, "Let's go over to the other side."*
> ³⁶ *Leaving the multitude, they took him with them, even as he was, in the boat. Other small boats were also with him.*
> ³⁷ *A big wind storm arose, and the waves beat into the boat, so much that the boat was already filled.*
> ³⁸ *He himself was in the stern, asleep on the cushion, and they woke him up, and told him, "Teacher, don't you care that we are dying?"*
> ³⁹ *He awoke, and rebuked the wind, and said to the sea, "Peace! Be still!" The wind ceased, and there was a great calm.*
> ⁴⁰ *He said to them, "Why are you so afraid? How is it that you have no faith?"*
> ⁴¹ *They were greatly afraid, and said to one another, "Who then is this, that even the wind and the sea obey him?"*
> (Mark 4:35-41)

In these verses, we can see Jesus' authoritative power at work amid a storm. In verse 37, the storm Jesus and his disciples were traveling through was so tumultuous that water had started coming into the boat. Jesus, however, isn't in a state of panic, but displays remarkable calm. He was asleep in the boat, and had to be woken up by his disciples!

"Teacher, don't you care that we're going to drown?"

How could Jesus sleep through such a terrible maelstrom? Did He not care about the safety of His disciples, or even worse, His own safety? Of course, He did! Jesus could sleep because He recognized and was confident in His own power to command the wind and waves. When awakened by His disciples—not the storm itself—Jesus rebukes the wind and sea, then reprimands the men for their lack of faith during this demonstrative lesson. Jesus may have been asleep, but He was very much present and mighty in power.

Among the many lessons available from these verses, Jesus teaches the importance of speaking peace to the elements of a storm. In Mr. Washington's experience, his masterful presence was the key strategy in ensuring that a cafeteria of restless students didn't become a chaotic nightmare. In recognizing his power, Mr. Washington reminds us that we don't have to lose control or the respect of our students when exercising our authority as leaders.

Mr. Washington held fast to his expectations for his students. He made the choice to boldly address the misbehavior, reset expectations, and move forward toward the greater goal of learning. Although Mr. Washington expressed disappointment when his students did not initially meet his expectations, he refused to allow it to deter him from the greater plans he had for them. His actions mirror those of the Master Teacher who was leading His students to cross over the sea because of the greater works and lessons He had planned.

An educator's prayer:

Lord, I believe that you have given me authority to command your peace in every situation. Help me to remain levelheaded and calm when I encounter disturbances in my professional environment, and to speak peace to every storm. In Jesus' name, Amen.

Notes:

4

TEACHING FOR UNDERSTANDING

Research has shown that using a tripartite strategy known as the Concrete, Representational, Abstract (CRA) sequence improves conceptual understanding and increases retention (Access Center, 2004).

In teaching mathematics, the sequence follows these steps: (1) introducing a concept with concrete objects or manipulatives, (2) guiding students into drawing or interpreting a representation, and (3) expressing the concept numerically or algebraically. Figure 1 provides a visual example of how the CRA method can be used to help a child understand the concepts of quantity and number.

An educator may help students understand the quantity of eight by having them demonstrate or "show" the value using blocks. In the *representational* phase, the same quantity is indicated as eight circles drawn on a whiteboard ten-frame. In the *abstract* phase, students can begin to associate the numeral "8" as the numeric form of the quantity they have previously been drawing and modeling with objects.

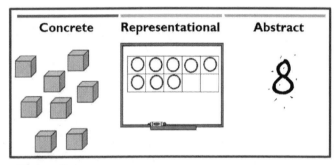

Figure 1

Unfortunately, some teachers only see the CRA sequence as being useful for elementary students, yet this instructional approach is significant for students of all grades and abilities. The CRA sequence isn't about "playing with materials" or "drawing pictures" to learn math; the method supports and guides how students think about the math they are learning.

The CRA sequence lays a practical groundwork to help us rationalize the intricate aspects of many foundational properties and conjectures.

Throughout the Old and New Testaments, we find evidence of God revealing His promises to His people through concrete, representational, and abstract sequences. Many Bible scholars believe that the acts of the New Testament are a revelation of the concrete actions depicted in the Old Testament.

In the life of Jesus, one of the many examples of this sequence can be seen through His sacrifice on the cross. Prior to Jesus' sacrifice, the people of God regularly used animals as sacrificial offerings to atone for sin. The blood of the sacrificial animal was a concrete offering repeatedly presented to God on behalf of the people for redemption of their sin.

Jesus, the Lamb of God, bore the sin of humanity on the cross, *eternally* providing forgiveness for our every sin before God. In addition to his death on the cross being a concrete sacrifice for humanity, Jesus also represents us before God. As a result, everyone who believes in Him has been promised everlasting life (John 3:16).

While we are not physically entering a temple to access the Most Holy Place or being sprinkled with the actual blood of Christ (Hebrews 10:19-23), we are still able to understand the spiritual, abstract implications of His sacrifice. Jesus shares with us that the Spirit of truth abiding in and with us cannot be seen and/or accepted by all men (John 14:17, 1 Corinthians 2:14), "and what we will be has not yet been made known" (1 John 3:2, New International Version). The Spirit of God helps us to understand how we are to become living sacrifices ourselves, and living epistles before men (Romans 12:1; 2 Corinthians 3:2).

As an educator, I find it fascinating that God would use the CRA sequence to reveal the realities of his existence and His plan for us. God is a master in scaffolding information so that we can learn more about Him. By faith, we can use these concrete and representational truths to grasp abstract knowledge of our lives and inheritance as sons and daughters of God.

Making the Connection

In the Apostle Paul's second letter to the church in Corinth, he shares examples from his own life and offers an explanation as to why God often uses scaffolding (laying one spiritual lesson upon another) as an instructional strategy to guide us into truth. In this sequence of learning about a spiritual truth, Paul begins his letter by expressing his desire to provide pragmatic instruction of God's master plan for humanity (2 Corinthians 2:1-3). He later explains how the teaching and acts of the Spirit of God are really "hidden", or abstract, to the human mind, and it is the mature believer who can understand the wisdom which is the mystery of God (2 Corinthians 2:6-8).

A concrete understanding of the things of God must be established before the abstract ideas of the Spirit even make sense to the human mind. As Paul writes, you must first receive the Spirit of God before you have the mind of Christ (2 Corinthians 2:14-16). In having the mind of Christ revealed to us, we are now able to understand the purpose of His great sacrifice, build on this knowledge and experience truth which previously seemed incomprehensible.

Throughout the course of their formal education in school, students are introduced to abstract ideas, which seem disconnected and meaningless unless their educational experience has included substantial coverage of the foundational material preceding it. To put it simply, it is unreasonable to expect students to *successfully* build upon knowledge that is either weak or nonexistent. Students should be presented with—and constantly see examples of—concrete and visual representations of the topics they are learning.

Unless a student truly has a solid foundation, future interpretations of more abstract concepts will be much like the spiritual knowledge of the immature believers in the Corinthian church: limited, irrational, and/or illogical.

An educator's prayer:

Lord, as I instruct and teach others, I pray that I would always remain teachable. Thank You for scaffolding my knowledge of

You, and being patient with me as I learn and grow. Help me to demonstrate the same level of attentiveness as I design and implement instructional activities for each of my students.

Guide me as I provide them with opportunities to establish a strong foundation of knowledge from which greater levels of comprehension can develop. Help me to remember the many examples of scaffolding You provide for me, so that I might be intentional in using and considering concrete and representational understandings related to my content to guide my students' knowledge of abstract ideas. In Jesus' name, Amen.

Notes:

5
DIFFERENTIATED INSTRUCTION

Differentiated instruction is an educational philosophy that recognizes all individuals learn differently and so teachers should actively seek ways to help students access their curriculum. Educational researchers and teachers suggest differentiation can take place by providing multiple avenues for acquiring content, varying the processes used for instruction, and allowing students to demonstrate their understanding through a variety of products.

In studying Jesus' life, we see pedagogical examples of the Master Teacher using various approaches to ensure all students could acquire the knowledge and skills He came to teach.

Jesus Teaches through Whole Group Instruction

Whole group instruction takes place when all students are involved in the same learning activity. While this approach to classroom instruction is disparaged by some, it is one which can be effective when used judiciously. Whole group instruction is traditionally identified as lecture-based or teacher-led, but can include a variety of methods—including tasks facilitated by students. For example, demonstrations led by a teacher or students, discussions with a large group, as well as explaining step-by-step instructions to the entire class about an upcoming task are all examples of whole group instruction (McLeod et al., 2003).

Jesus often utilized whole group instruction throughout his ministry as great crowds of people were always surrounding and following Him (Mark 5). When the woman with the issue of blood approached Jesus amid a large crowd (Mark 5:24-34), the lesson affirmed the power of exercising great faith.

In His sermon on the mount, the longest

continuous discourse of Jesus, He teaches *thousands* of men, women and children in one large setting (Matthew 5-7).

Jesus Teaches Through Small Group Instruction

> ³⁵ *While he was still speaking, people came from the synagogue ruler's house saying, "Your daughter is dead. Why bother the Teacher any more?"*
> ³⁶ *But Jesus, when he heard the message spoken, immediately said to the ruler of the synagogue, "Don't be afraid, only believe."*
> ³⁷ *He allowed no one to follow him, except Peter, James, and John the brother of James.*
> ³⁸ *He came to the synagogue ruler's house, and he saw an uproar, weeping, and great wailing.*
> ³⁹ *When he had entered in, he said to them, "Why do you make an uproar and weep? The child is not dead, but is asleep."*
> ⁴⁰ *They ridiculed him. But he, having put them all out, took the father of the child, her mother, and those who were with*

him, and went in where the child was lying.
⁴¹ Taking the child by the hand, he said to her, "Talitha cumi!" which means, being interpreted, "Girl, I tell you, get up!"
⁴² Immediately the girl rose up and walked, for she was twelve years old. They were amazed with great amazement. (Mark 5:35-42)

Some theologians believe that Jesus only invited Peter, James, and John to enter the home because the space was possibly too small for all the disciples to fit. Other theologians believe it was not a coincidence that Jesus invited these three men inside, as they were the closest to Him, and He wanted them to witness the miracle of raising this young woman from the dead— an opportunity for guided practice, as these three men would later be the only witnesses of His transfiguration (Matthew 17:1-13). What is clear about this decision is that Jesus was strategic in creating an instructional opportunity for a smaller group of individuals.

Jesus Teaches through Parables and Analogies

Differentiated instruction requires we honor the varying levels of experience and expertise students bring to the learning environment. Jesus differentiated lessons by teaching with parables based on individual learning needs.

Parables are stories used to illustrate a moral or spiritual lesson, and can promote values such as character, hard work and friendship. Teaching with parables can make certain ideas easier to understand and remember.

Over 40 of Jesus' parables are recorded in the Bible (Ahl, 2016), and many are related to the agricultural and economic standards of the times in which He lived. Jesus understood this was the background and experience of the people He came to teach, so these concepts were appropriate for many of the parables He taught. For example, the process of sowing seeds is often used to explain how the word of God is received in the hearts of different types of people (Matthew 13:3-23), and the story of the lives of various farmworkers is used to declare the acceptance of both Jews and Gentiles into the kingdom of God (Matthew 20:1-16). Analogies within the parables, such as those seen in the following passage, express a connection between common experiences and the kingdom of heaven:

[44] *"Again, the Kingdom of Heaven is like a treasure hidden in the field, which a man found, and hid. In his joy, he goes and sells all that he has, and buys that field.*
[45] *"Again, the Kingdom of Heaven is like a man who is a merchant seeking fine pearls,*
[46] *who having found one pearl of great price, he went and sold all that he had, and bought it.*
[47] *"Again, the Kingdom of Heaven is like a dragnet, that was cast into the sea, and gathered some fish of every kind,*
[48] *which, when it was filled, they drew up on the beach. They sat down, and gathered the good into containers, but the bad they threw away."* (Matthew 13:44-48)

As we see through Jesus' examples, differentiated instruction involves varying the *content* of what is being taught, the *process* by which it is taught, the expected *product* and even the learning environment to ensure students can access and interact with information at their level of ability, or their initial level of readiness.

God does not teach us – and does not love us – with a "one size fits all" approach.

We shouldn't teach our children that way either. His message was always the same, but His delivery changed based on the needs of each person He met.

An educator's prayer

Each of us is fearfully and wonderfully made in Your sight, Lord. Show me how to make this understanding a reality in how I teach. I believe You have given each child the ability to learn; teach me how to see and meet their needs. In Jesus' name, Amen.

Notes:

6
ENGAGE AND PERSEVERE

What is student engagement?

Student engagement is increasingly seen as an indicator of successful classroom instruction, and is increasingly valued as an outcome of school improvement activities. Students are engaged when they are attracted to their work, persist in [learning] despite challenges and obstacles, and take visible delight in accomplishing their work. Student engagement also refers to a "student's willingness, need, desire and compulsion to participate in, and be successful in, the learning process." (Fletcher, 2015)

It is extremely difficult to teach an individual who is socially, emotionally, or mentally disconnected from the learning environment. There are several external factors competing for students' attention every day, which can make the work of engaging them seem like an insurmountable challenge. As tough as it may be, it is not impossible, and requires persistence from the teacher and the student.

I was 21 years-old when I started my first full-time teaching position as a 5th grade teacher. Although I had many authentic teaching experiences and jobs in education, and obtained my degree in Mathematics Education prior to that assignment, nothing had really prepared me to teach the 28 extraordinary students I taught that year. I loved my students as if they were my own family; we laughed, cried, and fought like we were family too!

By February, I was quickly burning out. Low benchmark scores left me feeling inadequate as a teacher. I started to hate going to school, and even though I would work until 7 or 8 pm, and teach Saturday school, I started to believe the lie from the enemy that my students were never going to be successful. My memories of every triumph and accomplishment we made that year was fading fast as I started to focus on what wasn't working right.

I spent many afternoons tutoring Evan, a dedicated student whose reading and mathematics skills were 3-4 years below grade level. As we attempted another marathon of high-stakes testing drill and practice, I felt hopeless and lost my patience with him. At the end of our session, Evan and I were both exasperated. He packed his backpack, looked at me with a crestfallen gaze, then hung his head and mumbled, "Thank you, Ms. Ratliff" as he shuffled out of my classroom. My heart broke. I will never forget the look on his face or the sadness in his eyes.

In that moment, the Lord reminded me that Evan loved me, was committed to learning, and although progress was slower than *I* wanted, he was working just as hard as I was to engage himself in his studies. We were both persisting and striving towards the same goal, but I allowed feelings of failure and frustration to lead me to forget we were on the same team. I misjudged the situation and had to change my perspective. My students were counting on me to be as engaged and persistent as I was asking them to be.

Jesus expressed frustration with His disciples at various points during their journey together, but he still walked with them, taught them, and used them to accomplish mighty works throughout the earth. In Luke 5, Jesus approaches Simon (Peter) on his boat after he failed to catch any fish for an entire evening.

> *1 Now while the multitude pressed on him and heard the word of God, he was standing by the lake of Gennesaret.*
> *2 He saw two boats standing by the lake, but the fishermen had gone out of them, and were washing their nets.*
> *3 He entered into one of the boats, which was Simon's, and asked him to put out a little from the land. He sat down and taught the multitudes from the boat.*
> *4 When he had finished speaking, he said to Simon, "Put out into the deep, and let down your nets for a catch."*
> *5 Simon answered him, "Master, we worked all night, and took nothing; but*

at your word I will let down the net."
⁶ When they had done this, they caught a great multitude of fish, and their net was breaking.
⁷ They beckoned to their partners in the other boat, that they should come and help them. They came, and filled both boats, so that they began to sink.
⁸ But Simon Peter, when he saw it, fell down at Jesus' knees, saying, "Depart from me, for I am a sinful man, Lord."
⁹ For he was amazed, and all who were with him, at the catch of fish which they had caught;
¹⁰ and so also were James and John, sons of Zebedee, who were partners with Simon.

Jesus said to Simon, "Don't be afraid. From now on you will be catching people alive."
¹¹ When they had brought their boats to land, they left everything, and followed him. (Luke 5:1-11)

I can think of many days, months—even years—where I walked away from teaching feeling as if I failed to "reel in the catch" I had worked so tirelessly to obtain.

Although Simon was a fisherman by trade, we can relate to the frustration he must have felt when Jesus asked him to "put out into the deep" and try again. Because of his trust for Jesus, Simon willingly acts in accordance with His request. The results are staggering when you think about it: There was so much fish in that one catch that the boat began to sink. The even greater miracle was Jesus using his understanding of Simon's interests (fishing), a moment of failure, and the power of grit to engage him and ultimately transform his life.

Simon and his two business partners, James and John, left everything they had to follow Jesus. The challenge didn't deter them; the challenge drew them to Jesus because he showed them that their skills were valuable, that they could overcome failure, and led them to believe that anything was possible. Through this example, we understand Jesus can turn around our failures and make us successful in our work of reeling in students just like He did Peter in his work of reeling in fish.

The next time we feel weary, remember

that Jesus understands our frustration and wants us to remain steadfast in patient partnership so that we can experience the rewards of perseverance. God tells us His strength is made perfect in our weakness. God will give us the strength to engage our students and to persevere.

An educator's prayer

Lord, I desire to inspire and engage the students under my direction. I pray that I would be able to be persistent in the work You have called me to as an educator, and that I would see each student through Your eyes. Help me to not grow weary in well doing, for You have promised that I would reap if I faint not. I thank You for transforming the hearts and minds of every student I teach until they believe that all things are possible for them through Christ Jesus. In Jesus' name, Amen.

Notes:

7

INVESTING WITH EXPECTATION

Jesus uses the parable of the ten servants to highlight God's expectations regarding the gifts and talents each of us have been given.

11 As they heard these things, he went on and told a parable, because he was near Jerusalem, and they supposed that God's Kingdom would be revealed immediately.
12 He said therefore, "A certain nobleman went into a far country to receive for himself a kingdom, and to return.
13 He called ten servants of his, and gave them ten mina coins,[1] and told them, 'Conduct business until I come.'
14 But his citizens hated him, and sent an

---

[1] 10 minas were more than 3 years' wages for an agricultural laborer.

envoy after him, saying, 'We don't want this man to reign over us.'

¹⁵ *"When he had come back again, having received the kingdom, he commanded these servants, to whom he had given the money, to be called to him, that he might know what they had gained by conducting business.*

¹⁶ *The first came before him, saying, 'Lord, your mina has made ten more minas.'*

¹⁷ *"He said to him, 'Well done, you good servant! Because you were found faithful with very little, you shall have authority over ten cities.'*

¹⁸ *"The second came, saying, 'Your mina, Lord, has made five minas.'*

¹⁹ *"So he said to him, 'And you are to be over five cities.'*

²⁰ *Another came, saying, 'Lord, behold, your mina, which I kept laid away in a handkerchief,*

²¹ *for I feared you, because you are an exacting man. You take up that which you didn't lay down, and reap that which you didn't sow.'*

²² *"He said to him, 'Out of your own mouth will I judge you, you wicked*

servant! You knew that I am an exacting man, taking up that which I didn't lay down, and reaping that which I didn't sow.

²³ Then why didn't you deposit my money in the bank, and at my coming, I might have earned interest on it?'

²⁴ He said to those who stood by, 'Take the mina away from him, and give it to him who has the ten minas.'

²⁵ "They said to him, 'Lord, he has ten minas!'

²⁶ 'For I tell you that to everyone who has, will more be given; but from him who doesn't have, even that which he has will be taken away from him.
(Luke 19:11-26)

Jesus uses this parable to help the listener understand that people who wisely use what they are given by God will receive even more; and those who misappropriate what they are given by God will end up with less than the aforementioned individuals. Eventually, because of poor choices, those who misuse what they have been given will have the little they have left snatched away.

While a focus on financial management is important, the implications of misusing or undervaluing any gift cannot be lost on us. Teaching is a gift (Romans 12:7).

If teaching is a gift, and if making good use of your gift will cause it to exponentially increase, then how do you use it well?

When we make wise investments with our gifts, by faith, we *should* expect a return. I have taught and mentored children and young adults who faced horrific situations, but overcame abuse, death and major crises to experience major turnarounds in their lives. I have been a part of helping teachers and schools experience great academic gains and achievements. I have been a member of organizations who have made amazing strides in educational research and policy. I have experienced many years of success as an educator and leader because I began to understand the significance of what God had invested in me, and sought Him to learn more about how I was called to use my teaching gift.

It's easy to get excited about the financial concepts behind the idea of investments and increase, but at the core of the parable of the ten servants, Jesus reminds us it is a process which involves time, effort, risk and sacrifice. Investing in your gift as a teacher means choosing to be a life-long learner in fellowship with God. A good return on the investment requires abandoning selfish behavior, addressing your pride, and recognizing your need for others.

Defining the Master Teacher

¹ A shoot will come out of the stock of Jesse, and a branch out of his roots will bear fruit.
² Yahweh's Spirit will rest on him: the spirit of wisdom and understanding, the spirit of counsel and might, the spirit of knowledge and of the fear of Yahweh.
³ His delight will be in the fear of Yahweh. He will not judge by the sight of his eyes,

neither decide by the hearing of his ears; ⁴ but with righteousness he will judge the poor, and decide with equity for the humble of the earth. He will strike the earth with the rod of his mouth; and with the breath of his lips he will kill the wicked.
⁵ Righteousness will be the belt of his waist, and faithfulness the belt of his waist. (Isaiah 11:1-5)

In verse 2 of this prophecy, Isaiah describes the characteristics of the coming King, also known as the Master Teacher: wise, understanding, perceptive; One who provides prudent counsel, and is strong, knowledgeable, and intelligent. Have you asked the Holy Spirit to inspire you with the spirit of wisdom and understanding, the spirit of counsel and might, or the spirit of knowledge and the fear of the Lord? Investing in these attributes will increase the return and effectiveness of your gift.

An educator's prayer

Lord, help me to fully express the gifts You have given me while I am on this earth.

You have said I am Your workmanship, and have been created in Christ Jesus for good works that You prepared beforehand. Help me to rely on You and not struggle to complete this work in my own strength. Fill me with Your spirit of wisdom and understanding, the spirit of counsel and might, the spirit of knowledge and the fear of the Lord so that I may wisely use my teaching gift for Your glory. In Jesus' name, Amen.

Notes:

8

THE POWER OF WORDS

The job of an educator goes well beyond planning, delivering instruction and often into the zone of "other duties as assigned." We are on public display, and people not only respond to our actions, but the words we speak—and how we speak them—can leave an impression for the rest of their lives.

In Genesis 1:27, the author writes we have been created in the likeness of God, which means that we have the same characteristics He does. When God created the heavens and earth as recorded in Genesis 1, He did so by speaking things into existence. We, too, have been given the authority to create and destroy through the words which come out of our mouths, which is why we must be wise about what we say.

In the book of Proverbs, Solomon mentions the power of words and the tongue several times:

Death and life are in the power of the tongue; those who love it will eat its fruit. (Proverbs 18:21)

There is one who speaks rashly like the piercing of a sword, but the tongue of the wise heals.
(Proverbs 12:18)

Pleasant words are a honeycomb, sweet to the soul, and health to the bones.
(Proverbs 16:24)

He who guards his mouth guards his soul. One who opens wide his lips comes to ruin. (Proverbs 13:3)

In the book of Matthew, the writer describes a conversation between Jesus and a group of Pharisees and scribes, where the latter groups interrogated His disciples and claimed they dishonored the Jewish law. As Jesus counters their argument, He also clarifies an even more important issue for His disciples:

> 16-20 *Jesus replied, "You, too? Are you being willfully stupid? Don't you know that anything that is swallowed works its way through the intestines and is finally defecated? But what comes out of the mouth gets its start in the heart. It's from the heart that we vomit up evil arguments, murders, adulteries, fornications, thefts, lies, and cussing. That's what pollutes. Eating or not eating certain foods, washing or not washing your hands—that's neither here nor there."* (Matthew 15:16-20, The Message)

Why is it so important for us to have a clean heart and to watch our words? Because we have a responsibility to not injure others. The old phrase, "Sticks and stones may break my bones, but words will never hurt me" is an absolute lie. Words do hurt. As educators, we have a responsibility to teach truth, and encourage others to be their best.

When we understand the power in our

words, we will exercise care not to call someone "stupid" or a "fool" because they made a poor choice, or to speak destructive words over a situation when we are upset—we could be potentially cursing the very people and things we claim to care about.

The power of positive thinking and speaking is more than a trendy idea, it is a spiritual principle. Speak life over your environment, and expect things to change. They will.

Walking and Speaking in Love

> *16 Let the word of Christ dwell in you richly; in all wisdom teaching and admonishing one another with psalms, hymns, and spiritual songs, singing with grace in your heart to the Lord.*
> *17 Whatever you do, in word or in deed, do all in the name of the Lord Jesus, giving thanks to God the Father, through him.* (Colossians 3:16-17)

The words we speak should encourage and admonish each other to a place of maturity (1 Thessalonians 5:13-15).

An educator's prayer

Lord, I understand the power of life and death are in my tongue, and I pray that You would help me to be mindful about the words I speak. Reveal to me the intentions behind everything I think and say, and show me how to appropriately address my emotions so that I can use my tongue as an instrument for building. Keep me from fruitless conversations and gossip about my students and colleagues. In Jesus' name, Amen.

Notes:

9
CHECKING FOR UNDERSTANDING

Assessment is a valuable practice because they inform our instruction by letting us know the degree to which students have mastered what has been taught. A student's performance on any assessment is a unique combination of many variables:
- preparedness,
- innate abilities,
- the presence (or absence) of test anxiety,
- the testing environment,
- time allowed for testing, and
- advanced insight into the structure and format of the assessment

Because there are so many factors impacting student's success on any given assessment, we must equip them with a comprehensive and strategic toolkit.

Jesus was always assessing his disciples. It was an ongoing process, and He would check for understanding by evaluating their responses to different situations. Many times, He was disappointed in their responses, and would call them out for their lack of faith or shortsightedness, but He continued to prepare them for the greatest test of all: life after His physical death.

In Mark 8, Jesus was preparing His students' toolkit by explaining what would happen to Him in the future, and how those who follow Him should respond. Even after His death, the chief priests and the Pharisees recounted Jesus' words and teachings from his time of preparation to Pontius Pilate (Matthew 27:63-64). Jesus' instructions were straightforward and actualized well after his death.

Preparation for Spiritual Testing

Jesus, who underwent a test in the wilderness before beginning his teaching ministry understood how Satan tempts and attacks men. He used the knowledge to add to the disciples' toolkit; instructing them on Satan and how he operates in this world (John 8:43-44, John 10:10, Matthew 13:19). Satan is still using the same tactics and causing confusion in the lives of people today, but God has given us His Spirit, which is the answer for passing each test and trial we face while we are still living in this world.

He instructs us to be prepared for spiritual warfare.

In the sixth chapter of Ephesians, the apostle Paul uses the battle garments of a soldier to illustrate how we can prepare ourselves for the constant battle being waged against us in the spirit:

[10] *Finally, be strong in the Lord, and in the strength of his might.*
[11] *Put on the whole armor of God, that you may be able to stand against the wiles of the devil.*

12 For our wrestling is not against flesh and blood, but against the principalities, against the powers, against the world's rulers of the darkness of this age, and against the spiritual forces of wickedness in the heavenly places.

13 Therefore put on the whole armor of God, that you may be able to withstand in the evil day, and, having done all, to stand.

14 Stand therefore, having the utility belt of truth buckled around your waist, and having put on the breastplate of righteousness,

15 and having fitted your feet with the preparation of the Good News of peace;

16 above all, taking up the shield of faith, with which you will be able to quench all the fiery darts of the evil one.

17 And take the helmet of salvation, and the sword of the Spirit, which is the word of God;

18 with all prayer and requests, praying at all times in the Spirit, and being watchful to this end in all perseverance and requests for all the saints.

(Ephesians 6:10-18)

These spiritual tools are effective in every space of our lives—especially in the work of preparing students for success in their own lives.

An educator's prayer
Lord, I believe that I have been blessed with every spiritual blessing in the heavenly places because of my relationship with Jesus Christ. Help me to access every tool to empower and prepare my students for the many tests they face in my classroom and in life. Open my heart to receive Your instruction and direction so that I can guide them as You see fit. In Jesus' name, Amen!

Notes:

10
INSTRUCTIONAL COACHING

I believe instructional coaching is one of the most effective methods for improving teacher pedagogy and content knowledge. Instructional coaching destroys the closed-door philosophy of teaching, to create opportunities for accountability and collaboration. Through coaching, we can give and receive honest feedback about our teaching practices, and how we can best meet the needs of the students we serve. While coaches can function in a variety of roles, their primary responsibility is to support teacher development.

It is important to understand that instructional coaching goes beyond mentoring. When teachers can develop a trusting relationship with a person serving in a coaching role, a mutually beneficial partnership can develop. The instructional coach should have a solid understanding of how to support teachers in taking ownership of their professional growth.

This model is not exclusive to education, but instructional coaching requires a high level of specificity.

> *Coaching in the teaching profession, which is designed to scale up teaching expertise, must be much more specific. Coaches themselves need to be excellent teachers in the same discipline as the teacher being coached, able to provide situation-specific assistance adapted to that teacher.* (West & Staub, 2003)

The Master Teacher Coaching His Disciples

[7] He called to himself the twelve, and began to send them out two by two; and he gave them authority over the unclean spirits.
[8] He commanded them that they should take nothing for their journey, except a staff only: no bread, no wallet, no money in their purse,

⁹ but to wear sandals, and not put on two tunics.

¹⁰ He said to them, "Wherever you enter into a house, stay there until you depart from there.

¹¹ Whoever will not receive you nor hear you, as you depart from there, shake off the dust that is under your feet for a testimony against them. Assuredly, I tell you, it will be more tolerable for Sodom and Gomorrah in the day of judgment than for that city!"

¹² They went out and preached that people should repent.

¹³ They cast out many demons, and anointed many with oil who were sick, and healed them.

(Mark 6:7-13)

When Jesus sent the twelve disciples out to teach, it was only after they spent time observing His instruction, and receiving coaching on how to become teachers of the Gospel themselves. Before sending them out to the world, Jesus made sure all His disciples were empowered to heal, deliver, and teach as He was, yet their preparation was ongoing. The disciples returned to Jesus to share their experiences and continued to grow in their knowledge as He coached them (Mark 6:30). This is always a reminder for me of the importance of continuing education and professional development.

As Jesus nears the time of his crucifixion, He encourages His disciples to understand the fullness and eternal nature of His coaching relationship with God and with us.

8 Philip said to him, "Lord, show us the Father, and that will be enough for us."

9 Jesus said to him, "Have I been with you such a long time, and do you not know me, Philip? He who has seen me has seen the Father. How do you say, 'Show us the Father?'

10 Don't you believe that I am in the Father, and the Father in me? The words that I tell you, I speak not from myself; but the Father who lives in me does his works.

11 Believe me that I am in the Father, and the Father in me; or else believe me for the very works' sake.

12 Most certainly I tell you, he who believes in me, the works that I do, he will do also; and he will do greater works than these,

because I am going to my Father.
¹³ Whatever you will ask in my name, that will I do, that the Father may be glorified in the Son.
¹⁴ If you will ask anything in my name, I will do it. (John 14:8-14)

Jesus ultimately lets His disciples— and us—know that we are being coached so that we can do even greater works. His teaching is designed to be ongoing. In receiving instruction, we become greater educators.

An educator's prayer

Lord, as I am teaching and coaching others, help me to always remain teachable. Thank You for coaching and guiding me to live a life that is pleasing to You. I pray that Your Holy Spirit will continue to guide and inspire me to coach others in my profession with wisdom. In Jesus' name, Amen.

Notes:

11

SETTING EXPECTATIONS FOR EXCELLENCE

The first six weeks of a school year are often the most important because they set the tone for the rest of the year. The norms and expectations we set forth require consistent dedication and unending patience with our students and ourselves. The process of creating this disciplined environment can be challenging, but yields positive long-term results for everyone, because it creates a space for effective teaching and learning to happen.

In our professional, personal, and spiritual lives, discipline has far reaching benefits. Creating boundaries between work and home helped me to accomplish more than I ever had when I would work 60-hour weeks. Establishing better eating habits and not allowing myself to skip workouts when I felt stressed or tired, led to fantastic changes in my health and weight. Spending time meditating on the word of God in prayer, and fasting deepens my relationship with Him. Trusting in God's promises instead of myself helped me to heal from decades of pain and disappointment at the hands of others. Living a disciplined life requires effort, sacrifice, and obedience, but is extremely rewarding.

Another example of spiritual discipline can be seen in Jesus' instructions for his disciples early in their ministry.

Love for Enemies

27 "But to you who are listening I say: Love your enemies, do good to those who hate you, 28 bless those who curse you, pray for those who mistreat you. 29 If someone slaps you on one cheek, turn to them the other also. If someone takes your coat, do not withhold your shirt from them. 30 Give to everyone who asks you, and if anyone takes what belongs to you, do not demand it back. 31 Do to others as you would have

them do to you.
32 "If you love those who love you, what credit is that to you? Even sinners love those who love them. 33 And if you do good to those who are good to you, what credit is that to you? Even sinners do that. 34 And if you lend to those from whom you expect repayment, what credit is that to you? Even sinners lend to sinners, expecting to be repaid in full. 35 But love your enemies, do good to them, and lend to them without expecting to get anything back. Then your reward will be great, and you will be children of the Most High, because he is kind to the ungrateful and wicked. 36 Be merciful, just as your Father is merciful. (Luke 6:27-36, NIV)

Although the response Jesus provides is often the last thing we want to do when we are offended, there's no way to misinterpret what he is saying to His disciples. The expectations seem irrational, yet Jesus was continually teaching them that His ways are above ours, and living life at this level of discipline will always lead to better results.

When you think about how difficult it

feels to exhibit the type of discipline Jesus is asking us to display in Luke 6, you should know that this is how many youth and young adults feel about some of the rules we put into place for them. In our natural world, the disciplined individual who is respectful of the laws and of others would be defined as an upright citizen. Rules and expectations can help youth and young adults learn responsibility for themselves and others.

We ask students to align their actions to academic and behavioral standards because we understand the value of discipline. The concept of discipline and its rewards, however, did not originate in schools; for those who belong to Christ Jesus, it *starts* in the kingdom of God.

The Value of Biblical Instruction and Discipline

> [16] *The whole Bible[2] was given to us by inspiration from God and is useful to teach us what is true and to make us realize what is wrong in our lives; it*

---

[2] 2 Timothy 3:16 The whole Bible, literally, "Every Scripture."

straightens us out and helps us do what is right. ^{17} It is God's way of making us well prepared at every point, fully equipped to do good to everyone.
(2 Timothy 3:16-17, The Living Bible)

In 2 Timothy 3:16-17, Paul describes the compensation for living a spiritually disciplined life. The Word of God, was given to us to teach us so that we might display heavenly citizenship to others.

In John 1:14, the author declares Jesus *is* the Living Word, "the Word was made flesh, and dwelt among us" (KJV). When Paul describes the written Word of God in his second letter to Timothy, he is describing the characteristics and purpose of the Master Teacher as well.

Read 2 Timothy 3:16 once more, focusing on how *Jesus Christ* is the Living Word and the Master Teacher.

Truth allows us to see where we have fallen short in our lives, and directs us towards living on a straight path, which will help us to do what is right.

It is Jesus who has been given to us as the Master Teacher to instruct us in the truth.

Seedtime and Harvest

15 And the seeds that fell on the good soil represent honest, good-hearted people who hear God's word, cling to it, and patiently produce a huge harvest. (Luke 8:15, New Living Translation)

This verse, which is the end of Jesus' parable about the fate of seeds sown in various environments, shows us there is a patient partnership required along with a commitment to being disciplined in our process. No seed can produce a huge harvest without time, patience, and care.

An educator's prayer

Lord, You speak to me about the importance of living in excellence, and Your word constantly reminds me of why it is necessary to live a disciplined life. Help me to convey this important life lesson to my students. Open their eyes that they might see how and why it is vital for them to be disciplined in their academic studies, and how this discipline leads to even greater fruit in their lives. Help me to be more disciplined as a learner—seeking You through prayer, fasting, and setting aside more time with You to understand the value of our relationship. In Jesus' name, Amen.

Notes:

12

THE COMPANY WE KEEP

While we may not be able to control who we work with, we are able to control the level of interaction we have them.

Being an educator is a difficult job, and finding the right types of support can increase our professional and personal growth. If we are not careful, the advice and suggestions of critical people around us can lead to us to give up hope – to stop believing that we can make a difference in the lives and circumstances God has called us to impact.

When Jesus went to visit the city of Capernaum, he was challenged by the skepticism expressed by many of the city's residents. It is hard to believe that even though many people in His community recognized He was gifted, they still refused to believe in His authority as the Son of

God. But even in this atmosphere of disbelief—as religious leaders sat around being critical of Him—there were five men who chose to believe differently.

> *1 When he entered again into Capernaum after some days, it was heard that he was in the house.*
>
> *2 Immediately many were gathered together, so that there was no more room, not even around the door; and he spoke the word to them.*
>
> *3 Four people came, carrying a paralytic to him.*
>
> *4 When they could not come near to him for the crowd, they removed the roof where he was. When they had broken it up, they let down the mat that the paralytic was lying on.*
>
> *5 Jesus, seeing their faith, said to the paralytic, "Son, your sins are forgiven you."*
>
> *6 But there were some of the scribes sitting there, and reasoning in their hearts,*
>
> *7 "Why does this man speak blasphemies like that? Who can forgive sins but God alone?"*

> ⁸ *Immediately Jesus, perceiving in his spirit that they so reasoned within themselves, said to them, "Why do you reason these things in your hearts?*
> ⁹ *Which is easier, to tell the paralytic, 'Your sins are forgiven;' or to say, 'Arise, and take up your bed, and walk?'*
> ¹⁰ *But that you may know that the Son of Man has authority on earth to forgive sins"—he said to the paralytic—*
> ¹¹ *"I tell you, arise, take up your mat, and go to your house."*
> ¹² *He arose, and immediately took up the mat, and went out in front of them all; so that they were all amazed, and glorified God, saying, "We never saw anything like this!"* (Mark 2:1-12)

The paralytic man met Jesus because he surrounded himself with people who were willing to help him move beyond his limitations. Bishop T.D. Jakes (2013) says, "Don't hook up with people who comfort you in your crisis but won't carry you to your deliverance". There were many obstacles the men faced that day, but they collectively refused to quit, and exercised their faith in an amazing way.

An educator's prayer

Lord, when my circumstances seem impossible, help me to remember that You are with me, and I am never alone. Lead me to connect with individuals who have the faith to believe the impossible can be achieved, and will speak life into situations which appear to be hopeless. I pray that I would be tenacious in seeking Your truth, and believing all things are possible. In Jesus' name, Amen!

Notes:

13

GIVE IT YOUR ALL

²³ And whatever you do, work heartily, as for the Lord, and not for men, ²⁴ knowing that from the Lord you will receive the reward of the inheritance; for you serve the Lord Christ. (Colossians 3:23-24)

In a conversation with one of my close friends, who is also an educator, she shared with me her struggles concerning the lack of planning and organization she observes in her son's preschool program. The director of the program informed her that the children would be placed in learning groups, but was unable to explain what evaluative measures would be used to determine the group each child should be in. My friend was understandably concerned, and mentioned that in her experience, some children are misplaced and assigned to learning groups based on their behavior instead of their learning ability, and she wanted to ensure that this practice would not take place with her child or any other children in the classroom.

As she began to describe a formative assessment she developed to help the instructors determine what skills the children possess, I was amazed by her dedication, and reminded of how important it is to continue to set high expectations for ourselves as educators as well as our students. What my friend was expressing through our conversation and her desire to see a change in the instructional delivery was, "I want to ensure the educators responsible for teaching my son and his classmates are giving their all."

When we commit to setting higher standards for ourselves, and raising the academic and behavior expectations for every student, the outcome should be classrooms and learning spaces where everyone is committed to excellence.

In Matthew 22, Jesus answers a Pharisee who asks him about the most important law, to which He responds by explaining how we should demonstrate excellence through our love for others.

> *34 But when the Pharisees heard that he had silenced the Sadducees, they gathered together.*
> *35 And one of them, a lawyer, asked him a question to test him.*
> *36 "Teacher, which is the great commandment in the Law?"*
> *37 And he said to him, "You shall love the Lord your God with all your heart and with all your soul and with all your mind.*
> *38 This is the great and first commandment.*
> *39 And a second is like it: You shall love your neighbor as yourself.*
> *40 On these two commandments depend all the Law and the Prophets."*
> (Matthew 22:34-40)

These commandments exhort us to love God with everything we have, and to love others with excellence.

J. Hampton Keathley (2009) says, "pursuing excellence is a matter of the heart, of the inner person and proceeds from an inner faith/relationship with God."

An educator's prayer

Father, I pray that You would continue to renew my strength and give me both the eyes to see You and ears to hear from You as I pour out my life for the work of teaching Your children.

Help me to remember that while I am working unto You, I am not working alone, and you have called me to love you and others with an excellent love. In Jesus' name, Amen!

Notes:

Bibliography

Ahl, Dave (2016). Jesus' 46 Parables in Chronological Order Christian Bible Study ~ Introduction and 26 Lessons. Retrieved from http://swapmeetdave.com/Bible/Parables/

Allen, S., Goddard, Y. (2010). Differentiated Instruction and RtI: A Natural Fit. Educational Leadership. Volume 68, Number 2. Retrieved from http://www.ascd.org/publications/educational-leadership/oct10/vol68/num02/Differentiated-Instruction-and-RTI@-A-Natural-Fit.aspx

Bible Hub. Bible Timeline http://biblehub.com/timeline/

Fletcher, A. Soundout (2015) Defining Student Engagement: A Literature Review. 29 March 2015 https://soundout.org/defining-student-engagement-a-literature-review/

Henry, Matthew. "John Chapter 1." http://www.biblestudytools.com/commentaries/matthew-henry-complete/john/1.html

Jakes, T.D. (2013, October 13) I Got This. Sermon presented at the Potter's House of Dallas in Dallas, TX.

Jakes, T.D. (2016, January 10) Being Grounded in Your Faith. Sermon presented at the Potter's House of Dallas in Dallas, TX.

Jakes, T.D. (2016, February 7) Grounded in Friends, Part 2. Sermon presented at the Potter's House of Dallas in Dallas, TX.

Keathley, J. H. (2009). Marks of Maturity: Biblical Characteristics of a Christian Leader. "Mark 11: The Pursuit of Excellence" https://bible.org/seriespage/mark-11-pursuit-excellence

McLeod, J., Fisher, J., Hoover, G. (2003). The key elements of classroom management: Managing time and space, student behavior, and instructional strategies. Alexandria, VA: Association for Supervision and Curriculum Development.

National Baptist Publishing Board (1977). *The New National Baptist Hymnal.* Triad Publications.

The Access Center (2004). Concrete-Representational-Abstract Instructional Approach. Retrieved from http://165.139.150.129/intervention/ConcreteRepresentationalAbstractInstructionalApproach.pdf

Tomlinson, C. A. (August 2000).

Differentiation of Instruction in the Elementary Grades. ERIC Digest. ERIC Clearinghouse on Elementary and Early Childhood Education. http://files.eric.ed.gov/fulltext/ED443572.pdf ERIC Identifier: ED443572

West, L., & Staub, F. C. (2003). Content-focused coaching: Transforming mathematics lessons. Portsmouth, NH: Heinemann.

What Works Clearinghouse (WWC) (2009). Assisting Students Struggling with Reading: Response to Intervention (RtI) and Multi-Tier Intervention in the Primary Grades.

Winfield, P. (2014, June 4). Bible Study presented at The Potter's House of Dallas in Dallas, TX.

Winston, B. (2017, August 27). Restoring the Years. Sermon presented at The Potter's House of Dallas in Dallas, TX.

ABOUT THE AUTHOR

Brea C. Ratliff has taught elementary, middle, high school, community college and university graduate courses. With a background in mathematics education, she has also been a Math/Science Academic Coach, K-12 District Mathematics Supervisor, and a Secondary Mathematics Education Research Coordinator.

Brea is the founder of Me to the Power of Three, (metothepowerof3.com), a consulting company focused on designing programs and resources to benefit K-12 learners. She is currently the President of the Benjamin Banneker Association, Inc., a national organization committed to ensuring African-American students achieve parity in mathematics education.

Brea is also an accomplished curriculum writer and a musician.

Made in the USA
Columbia, SC
06 September 2018